∞

Rubber
Rocketship

Rubber Rocketship

A Very Short Story of Love, Loss & Eternity

Argus Gray

DISILLUSIONMENT PRESS
USA / WORLDWIDE

for those who dare to love ...

despite the inevitability of loss

"Higher ... higher!"

she cried out in her shrill voice—
two parts, sheer joy ... one part, pure terror.

"I want to go higher!"

I thrust out my hands throwing my full weight into the swaying pendulum hanging above the *not so mighty* waters of Hinders Creek—the closest thing we had to an actual river in the small rural town Cinnamon and I called home.

Worn and sun cracked, the Michelin cradling
Cinnamon Taylor heaved itself into outer space.

What was once a front tire on Farmer O'Steen's
John Deere, had been transformed two summers
ago, into the sacred vessel now responsible
for transporting my love up to the stars.

A rubber rocketship that carried not one,
but two hearts, to the heavens and suspended
them there, without worries or dread of what
the earth below would one day ask of them.

The evening air was cool, like the waters we had swam in throughout the heat of the afternoon.

We had kissed that day, a simple kiss spurred on by the unexpected appearance of a coral snake slithering along the creek bed.

Jumping back into the waiting safety net of my arms, we bumped heads, and while laughing and crying—we kissed for the first time.

"Push me again… I want to go higher!"

As the swing, made of rubber and rope,
descended toward me in a downward arc,
I raised my hands and recoiled my arms to
ready myself for another shove.

Then suddenly, without warning,
I felt compelled to hold back some of my
brimming adolescent strength.

I feared what would happen
if I pushed too hard—c*ould she go too high*…
too far into a world I didn't know,
a world, I wasn't yet prepared to enter?

"I'm flying!"… she cried, *"I'm flying!"*

Her laughter, so unabashed, mixed with
the flowing waters to form a love song.

"I know!" I shouted—
and, *I love you*… I whispered.

She didn't hear me.

A sudden grip tightened on my hand, rousing me from my daydream.

"I'm flying," she said.

I opened my eyes and saw the girl I kissed...
who became the woman I loved... the mother of
our wonderful and amazing children.

Random memories of immense joy
began to flood my tired mind.

Over the years, we had travailed through
both light and darkness, yet her beauty
remained untarnished by time, or even now...
by the cancer that filled her body.

I caressed the few remaining wisps
of golden hair left atop her scalp.

Again, it was she that would venture into
the unknown... and I, afraid to let her go.

Her face, pale and gaunt, managed a soft smile.
"I'm flying," she whispered, as her eyes closed.

"Yes, I know you are..."
I whispered back,

".. and, I love you."

Our hands still clasped, I swam in the silence,
not wanting to let go of this moment.

And, while I can't be sure that
she heard the last words I spoke to her,
I was certain this time... *she knew.*

Love never ends…
it dwells in a Universe… without time.

∞

About the Author

Argus Gray is the name given to
a boy who has never grown up.

Whether it's because he can't...
or because he won't... is still unknown.

His physical body resides in Upstate NY,
driving his beautiful wife, Lenore, nuts from
his A.D.D. and erratic mood swings.

The rest of him...
lives happily in his own small mind...

.. writing quick read books for an A.D.D. generation,
and telling stories to whoever will listen.

Also by Argus Gray

Wake Up & Live!
How To Conquer The Rip Van Winkle Syndrome

Suicidal Thoughts

Who Am I?
A Simple Riddle That When Solved Answers
the Age Old Question We All Ask Ourselves...

Did You Know "Richard Cory"?

The Book of Truth
.. And Lies

If I Could Travel Through Time

Do You Know...
7 Simple Thoughts to Help You Awaken

Sleeping In The Trees
The Secret World of Princesses & Princes

Contact Argus Gray at:

www.argusgray.com

argusgray@gmail.com

Watch Argus Gray online at:

www.grayatnight.com

YouTube Channel: GrayatNight

www.ingramcontent.com/pod-product-compliance
Lightning Source LLC
Chambersburg PA
CBHW071747020426
42331CB00008B/2205